AF580845

Silver Century

Also by the author:

Crimson Dawning
Purple Petals
Silver Century (1936)
West to Glory
Her Majesty, Nevertheless

Silver Century

by Leola Christie Barnes

Illustrations by Eugene Haley

The Naylor Company
Book Publishers of the Southwest
San Antonio, Texas

Library of Congress Catalog Card No. 73-9204

Printed in the United States of America

ISBN 0-8111-0513-X

Dedicated

to

Four Sons of Texas
My husband, W. F. Barnes,
and my sons,
Joe, Billy and Jimmy

Acknowledgments

Home and Abroad, English Review, Poetry Studies, Woman's National Forum, Famous Poets and Poetry, New York Times Journal, Texas Anthology, New Zealand Woman's Weekly, Poems of the Nations, Personalities of Today, Crimson Dawning, Kansas City Journal.

Foreword

Poets, the creators of beauty, take the commonplace and make of it something indefinably exquisite. They are blessed with eyes that see beneath the surface of ordinary life, so that they live in a world of rainbow tints, sublimated with the majesty of mountain crags and luminous with storm-swept skies.

Mrs. Leola Christie Barnes, possessing this colorfully creative soul to an amazing degree, has forever enriched the realms of literature in her new volume, *Silver Century*.

This striking book of poems, written in honor of the first hundred years of Texas life, is tuned to the "thunder of cowhide whips" which accompanied the "crunching wagon wheels that slowly ground their virgin route across the blue uncertainty of everlasting time to make a home of that daredevil west."

Silver Century holds the reader spellbound with its vivid resurrection of the mighty adventures and supreme sacrifices of our ancestors. The Declaration of Texas Independence has become a poem of "Kings in homespun jeans" who scratch their names with quill pens to that immortal document that made the "Land of the Tehas" a Lone Star State of America.

This Texas author, who is a native daughter in the truest sense of the word, has reglorified her famous poem, "A Cotton Picker" over and over again in

Silver Century. Time and again the rumbling of oxen-drawn wagons and gaunt men on leathery horses traverse the paths of our hearts as we see them transforming a wilderness into an alluring and peaceful commonwealth.

It gives me pleasure to congratulate Mrs. Barnes on her fine contribution to the best literature of our time and to commend this volume of verse as a fitting souvenir of our Lone Star Centennial.

Pat M. Neff, A.M., L.L.B., LL.D.

President of
Baylor University,
Ex-Governor of Texas

Contents

A Texas Century 2
Saint Denis 4
Obstetrics 5
The Land of the Tehas 6
A Texas Explorer 8
Fathers of Texas 9
West Texas 10
Discovers Texas 12
Old San Antonio Road 14
Mission San Francisco of the Tehas 16
Philip Nolan 17
Mothers of Texans 18
San Antonio 20
Making Home 22
Gonzales 23
Texas Fathers 24
Life and Death 25
Texas Today 26
Silver Trekkers 28
La Salle 30
Pioneer City 31
Old Spanish Trail 32
To Washington-on-the-Brazos 33
Alamo of Today 34
The Court Oak 36
Little House 37

Martyrs 38
Recollection 39
Trial of Kiowa Chief 40
Texas 41
Litany of Cottonwoods 42
Life 43
Song of the Paluxy 44
Gallantry 47
Tanka of Faith 48
Lifted with a Song 49
Quiescence 50
Mystic of Grand Canyon 51
Song of a Dying Hopi 52
A Sandstorm 53
Reply to William Shakespeare 54
Gypsy Night 55
Mortality 56
Geraniums 57
To a City 58
Beauty in Grief 59
Early Bug 60
A Nightitude 61
Autumn Speaks 62
Tarantula 63
Penitence 64
Silver Wedding Anniversary 65
Friend 66
Gins 67
Paulina 68
Earth Fools 69
My Emergency Kit 70
Lupez 71
An Easterner Describes a Ranch 72
Evanescence 73

Ingratitude 74
San Angelo 75
My Mustang 76
Spring Out West 77
Old Bill 78
Monarch of the Plains 79
Cowboy Song 80
Isidro the Shepherd 81
Da Americano 82
To a Writer Friend 83

Illustrations on pages 1, 3, 7, 11, 13, 15, 19, 21, 27 and 35

Silver Century

A Texas Century

Hewn from the dust of the ages
And visions of leather men;
A changing land of promise,
Of palace and cattle pen.

A land of despair and fulfillment,
A land where the mockingbird sings,
Where bluebonnets glow on the hillsides,
Touched by the whir of wings.

Over her thirsting prairies
The wind in torrents sweep,
And giants of memory are watching
Where the dreams of heroes sleep:

Her Goliad, Gonzales, and Austin,
Her Alamo, her Bowie, her light,
Her longhorns, her iron, her Houston,
Her glory, her star, and her might.

And you, who have not loved her,
This wilful, this lavish land,
Cannot know the depths of her caring,
Nor the grip of her friendly hand;

But He, who made the centuries,
Made home, and will understand.

Hewn
From
The
Dust
Of the ages
And visions of
leather
men;
A changing land of promise
Of palace
and
cattlepen.

Saint Denis

On and on his words are flowing, silver dipped,
Bassanio of all he surveys.
Saint Denis with fever in his breast and pallid lipped,
But feigns to strut. "There sways
The maiden land of the Tehas,
A virgin dying for me.
My love shall make chaos
Of her dimples. Hasinai shall see.

A virgin clothed in antelope and muted horns that
flame
With chance is panting at my door. . . ."
His quenchless fire and trifles came
To the arrowed village, where enraged score
On score of color swooped on him
With hellish barbs of joy.
The silken lover in grim
Delight embraced them as a toy.

Obstetrics

Glamorous Tehas!
Home and chance!
Torn apart
By Spain and France.
Thunder peals!
Kings turn pale
At wagon wheels.
A cabin built,
A row of corn,
A patchwork quilt.
A state was born.

The Land of the Tehas
(Described by Cabeza de Vaca)

I stood transfixed before her magnitude, oh, King!
Celestial beasts with horns as trees are tall
Reclined on satin grass. Beyond I saw a glittering
Of magic palaces and every wall
A fire, with beams of precious gold
Aslant with jewels. Her splendor cannot be told.

The natives? Ah! Angels with feathered wings
Designed from rainbows. Cherubic things
Illumined the trees and blinked with godly eyes
Truly, King, you can be ruler of Paradise!

A Texas Explorer

The viceroy
Sent Coronado
To search
For the cities
Of fabulous glow.

Fathers of Texas

Through wilderness
And blood
They came,
Beating out pathways
To the sun,
Unawakened gorge
And trail,
Prairie land
And holy grail.

West Texas

(Described by Coronado)

I stepped into another world,
Vast and indescribable
In its charm;
Like a mighty mystery unfurled
For men to marvel at, and storm.

Not a hill to the east of me,
Not a hill to the west,
Nor north, nor south
Was anything but an open mouth
That seemed to swallow me,
And still, I felt the mystery.

Discovers Texas

He sailed too far
To the westward
And landed on Lavaca Bay;
He was forced
To settle in Texas
For wild gods
Blocked his way.

La Salle sailed too far west
And landed on the shore of Lavaca Bay;
He was forced to settle in Texas,
For strange lords blocked his way.

Old San Antonio Road

You ran ahead of our fathers,
Old road,
And like a flame of wind
You swept away
Devouring interludes
Of dismay,
And lifted men above a load
Of pitiful yearnings
And homesick burnings,
Into the trail of dawn.

You flaunted a blossom of scarlet cerise
For Ramon,
And bore three cities of starsome glow:
Bastrop,
Crockett,
San Antonio,
And like a flower
In the dawn,
You blossomed
On and on
Into the centuries.

Mission San Francisco of the Tehas

Coronado's explorations are followed by Father Massinet, who builds the first Texas church.

Who are these with muscles of brawn,
Hewing with axes the virgin trees,
Touched by the golden wings of dawn,
And armed with sabers? Who are these?

They are the sons of an opal land,
Who have dared to kindle a birth
Of golden light. To hold a hand
To the little ones of earth.

They carved from the wilds of the Tehas,
From the voices of bird and tree
A sun: a torch of promise
To illumine a century.

Philip Nolan

A hundred soldiers swing to arms
At sight of Philip Nolan;
His head is bare,
His heart is there
Where storms of passion
Beat his breast.
Who are you to dare
Philip Nolan?

"Come on, my foes,
God knows
That I am Philip Nolan."

A hundred bullets pierce the air
And stain the hair
Of Philip Nolan.

Lay him to rest —
The first of Texas martyrs —
The brave grass stirs
Above the breast
Of Philip Nolan.

Mothers of Texans

Gaunt with the strength of courage,
Grim in the presence of death,
She reigned a goddess of beauty
In her log cabin home. A breath
Of spring in her laughter; a viking soul
In her breast; she toiled and sang and lifted
To make home of that daredevil west.
To die for her children's children
Was the song that she loved best.

San Antonio

(1730)

A million shining angels stood
Where yesterday had been a wood,
And carved an infant town —
San Fernando de Bexar!
A sun went down,
A moon revealed an Alamo
White and still
And all around
A mission hill;
Above a grayer,
A holier ground
That rose into a flaming crown
Of gloryhood.

Making Home

Hearth fires glow
From flint
And steel
And trundle beds
Where mothers kneel.

Gonzales

A stern-mouthed cannon
Split the dawn
And jarred her rumbling wheels
Beneath a stench of nausea
And flying Mexican heels.
Gonzales,
Lone Star Lexington,
Unsheathed a sword
That cried to earth,
And clipped the cord of Texas' birth.

Texas Fathers

Ragged kings in homespun jeans
Removed their crowns of raccoon hide,
Dipped their sceptered pens in blood,
Sketched eternity — and died.

Life and Death

A blood-red banner
Floats from Bexar;
The Texas brave are there
To lift a star
Above the tide
Of death
They deified.

Texas Today

A state as luminous as the fiery sun,
And honor and the crimson tide
Of patriots' blood so fiercely rung
From hearts that groanless died.
Each sceptered point is a bleeding flame
Of a gallant hero's love,
Who gave a life for a land to live
In the glow of a star above.
It touched the heavens and centered there,
A luminary for nations great:
A star transmuted to shine abroad,
A replica of our state.

HOMESEEKERS

The thunder of cowhide whips
Shattered the stillness,
And crunching wagonwheels
Slowly ground a virgin route
Across the blue uncertainty
Of everlasting time.
Men of gaunt design,
They guided their stolid oxen
As God was guiding them,
Ever westward.
Hearts of man and beast
Grew tense with watching
For the evening star
And home.

Silver Trekkers

(A Sestina)

The dangers of interminable scope
Surrounded them, those giants of sun-drenched plains
Who trekked into unknown despair and won
The thundering applause of gods and men.
No martial music greeted them but cries
Of starving wolves and scars where rattlers trilled.

They laughed at bleaching bones where death had
trilled
Her song to howling winds that dyed her scope
With crematory dust. They heard the cries
Of prairie dogs as ghouls of phantom plains,
But only living gods could touch these men
Whose haggard forms had fought with hell and won.

When winding April saw that they had won
She scattered victor buds and songsters trilled
Their prairie hymns to thankful hearts of men
Amazed to see the miracle of silver scope
That surged its waves across the mighty plains
Attuned to melodies of welcome cries.

They learned to love the music of the cries
That smote the nights and lulled their sleep; new-won
Mesquites of downy green adorning plains
With twinkling fans of lace where bluebirds trilled
Doxologies to him who gave this scope
Of new America to singing men.

When autumn came she found her leather men
In cow camps; wild mustangs had heard their cries
Of victory and wildly circled the scope
Of whirling hemp outflung by hands that won.
Adobe huts appeared and children trilled
Their songs to laughter of the plains.

They quaffed the chalice of sirens as plains
Transformed the dreams of pioneering men
And held aloft the courage angels trilled
To hearts of singing puritans. The cries
Of death were dares to those whose fathers won
America and charmed this western scope.

ENVOY

Eternal plains of God extol the cries
Of pioneering men who dared and won
A land that trilled their dreams of silver scope.

La Salle

Mystery keeps a silver wall
Around the hallowed name, La Salle.
The sun's lean daggers guard his rest
As cadent breezes from the west
Whisper softly while they fall.

Thin April rain comes to appall
Time's sacred nocturnes that enthrall
The greatness of him whose quest
Mystery keeps.

Golden galleons of years attest
The eternal glory, whose crest
Touches the stars, and children call
Your name in school, fearless La Salle.
Martyred father, the wall is best
Mystery keeps.

Pioneer City

San Antonio
If dust could speak
The air would reek
And tales would flow.

War whoops and prayer
Were blended. No,
A priest was there
And bending low.

Siestas kissed
Away the hate
That arrows missed
Inviolate.

Another sound,
The Alamo!
A flaming mound,
An afterglow.

Mere dust can talk
For tourist quaff
Your air and walk
Along and laugh.

Old Spanish Trail

A road that heard the fiery tread of faith,
The clank of swords, the buccaneeric songs,
Now bears the grinding shriek of brakes. A wraith
Of Ponce de Leon, aghast when throngs
Of tourists honk, discards his wings of youth,
And hollow eyed, retreats to where La Salle
With Gallic sword, once came in search of truth.
Now maddened tribes dash by and sunbeams fall.

A trail of stars looks down amazed; a crone
Is begging alms where Houston once went by
In fleeting wrath, undaunted and alone.
There tramped, with flaming swords and faith held
 high,
Conquistadors and iron men, who found
An Alamo and this enchanted ground.

To Washington-on-the-Brazos

Unceasing lash of silver time nor pain
Of silent glory can destroy the song
I sing of altar dust and you. Along
The Brazos chimes a desolate refrain
Of Old Republic. Cloistered worlds contain
Our fathers whose hands built your crumbling walls
That tremble slightly when a red bird calls
A challenge to earth and emerald rain.

No regal pomp nor military tread
Disturbs the majesty of your dear past.
Within proud hearts we hold your lofty dead
And lift our hands to you for deeds now past:
A document was written where you stand,
Immortal spot, that bore a Fatherland.

Alamo of Today

They walk with cadent steps into the shrine
That heard the muttered threats of swarming foes
And saw their bloody carnage; felt the blows
Of martyred men. Along incarnadine
Partitions tourists talk of Travis' line;
Of Bowie's courage that defied the rows
And ranks of Mexicans. A crevice glows
With blood that marks a sacrificial sign.

The mission fort is now unbarred to all
The curious invading throng, who seek
The line that Travis made, and knowing call
Their sons to see the spot. In awe they speak
Of blood where sunbeams tiptoe in to meet
The shades of victors and hurrying feet.

The Court Oak *

Lamenting tourists seek your skylit shade
Columbus Oak, but fail to see the one
Who stood with lifted head, who fought and won
Our dearest liberty with love he laid
Upon an altar. Pierced and unafraid
He built a state on wounds and prison bars
That quenched the tide of everlasting wars
And hallowed those who suffered, fought and prayed.

And you have stood unscathed by blood and flame
As centuries have bared their hearts to you,
Sometimes in triumph and sometimes in shame.
Where are the brave years that Austin knew
Of living struggle, silent hopeful pain
That taught his sons to hope and pray again?

---

* (This huge live oak, a thousand years old, stands in Columbus, Texas. Under its shade was held the First District Court of Texas by Stephen F. Austin, Father of Texas.)

Little House

Little house with the golden light
Peeping through the trees tonight,
Your inmates were born of the charging foam,
The shifting prairies were once their home
As they trekked the wilds by oxen drawn
And with courage of gods went proudly on
Pierced by the arrows of earth and hell,
Disease and drouth and savage yell.
So little house with the golden light
Be proud of the sons you shelter tonight.

Martyrs

A motley throng
Of tourists from the street
Desire to see
Where mortal heroes fought
To death for them.

Expanding with conceit
Of native pride
They talk of states blood bought,
Of one who asked
Of men to lift his cot.
But once outside
They murmur, "O how hot!"

Recollection

We loitered along the highway
Romance and memory and I
Until the wheels of yesterday
Were slowly grinding by.

Trial of Kiowa Chief

Rigidly alert
To every move
He stood in chains
And savage hate before
The Texas court.

"Me prove
Me heapa big chief
And love Tehanna;
Me bear the taunts
Of my tribe
Who say me squaw
Because me love Tehanna.

I suffer now
For crimes of those
Bad ones: Black Pow Wow,
Eagle Heart and Coyose.

If you will let me go
I will wash out the spots of blood
And make the hearts
Of my people white as snow."

They saw a scalping knife
Hidden under savage bravado
And understood.
They asked his life.

Texas

I love you, golden Texas,
Land of horn and hoof and plain
With your voice of uncurbed freedom,
Jingling spur and bridle rein.

Where other states have courtly halls
Liveried men and brown stone walls,
You have shacks, adobe huts
And the lowing cattle ruts.

Where other states have blooded sports
Royal heritage and courts,
You have felt the crescent dart
Of a stampede through your heart.

I love you, golden Texas,
Jingling spur and bridle rein,
With your uncurbed song of freedom,
"Men are brothers here," refrain.

Litany of Cottonwoods

O to ride over the prairies in spring
On my galloping pony, Carlotte,
And listen to blue quail a-westering
And sniff the fragrance of sweet berganot.

O to be there on a morning in May
And to feel the west winds on my throat,
I would give all of France and her grand soiree
For the lonely bark of a rangey coyote.

My lover rides there in his chaps and his boots
With a sombrero that crowns him a king
Of all others at roundups where all are "cahoots"
And "Little Dogie" is the song that they sing.

I can hear the litany of cottonwood trees
In silvered tones and the brimming cheers
Of wheels that turn and turn in the breeze,
Lover, I hear, for my heart has ears.

Life

White anemones,
Small beneath the rowan trees,
Evening primroses,
Budding hawthorn in a bed
Live in cities of the dead.

Song of the Paluxy

A harvest moon in saffron mauve
Inverted its crescent glow at dawn
And my dusky children laughed
And chanted hymns of praise among
The fluted peppermints that hung
Above my winding crystal path.

Millions of rainbow flowerlets glow
As Awon-aw-lona paints a bow
Of silver and hangs it gleaming high
Above the wigwams across the sky.

To glimmering gods of rain they fling
The sacred meal of earth and spring.

Swishing arrows leave a sparkling flame
That baffles the fireflies in their game
And mirrors the brothers of sunrays here
As my waters gurgle and disappear.

I sing of Nacona subtle and brave
Anointed with perfume of towering youth
And proud as the eagle when cloudlets wave
Their frosty banners across his booth.

Shining gods of the sun they wait for you
Over the Big Sea Waters they watch for you,
Wahbegwannee, the white Star Flowers
Will guide you.

II.

Fiestas of summer are chiming a tune
Of welcome to gods with shining hair
Who came in the full October moon
Across the churning waters. They were fair
As morning when they sailed beneath the gate
Of rainbows to where my awed ones await.

My children are planting prayer plumes
And scattering their whitened meal
To spirit gods of the woodland.
And all the gods of water and earth
Are kneeling to gods of the sun
And still they are coming.

Nacona speaks and the sun appears
Unfolding a dearth of summer tears.
I sing of golden pebble stones
Of gods in search of dreams,
Father of Waters conceal their moans
And save their rippling streams.

III.

The gods are thundering with firesticks,
Brave Nacona must sing the death song
To his lone brother the oak tree.

A sultry moon derisively peers
Above the headland of mountain dews
Revealing immortal tears
Of Nacona and weeping clouds suffuse
The dying stars.

Where are my dusky children,
My children of youth and flowers?
They sing in happy hunting grounds
Of deer and silver showers.

The gaunt refrain of a solitary knell
Clanged the hollow notes of autumn
And the ghastly funeral bell
Is tolling, tolling.

Beneath my troubled waters I hear
Nacona calling, calling from a stone.
O how long, my children
Must I be left alone?

Gallantry

The August world was petulant from heat,
Insipid with despair of dying herbs,
The valleys palpitated with whole suburbs
Of scarlet hills that swayed on blistered feet.
The rowdy wheels of traffic wore concrete
Into ascending dust that brazenly
Allied itself to high mahogany
In butlered homes and wagged along the street.

It burned — a yellow candle into night —
And earth became as brass in caldron flame
And cattle lowed and people flounced about,
"Too hot to sleep," they murmured with affright
As August drooped her crimson head in shame;
A gallant breeze arose and blew the candle out.

Tanka of Faith

A dying savage
Leaned against a tree and sang
Hozannas to God
And praised Him for a heaven
That beckoned to Him with stars.

Lifted with a Song

Her soul was sensitive to beauty, quick
To feel the bleary barbs of sorrow, yet
It was ashes of grief insistent, thick
That taught her heart to sing and to forget.
When poised for sudden flight we saw her fret
And fume at life and laugh derisively
At fate and heaven and boast that she
Could walk alone without a bayonet.

Then tragedy with all her gloomy train
Inflicted her until perdition wept
And her defense was broken. All day long
She called for death and swore that life was vain;
Then suddenly the god of love and faith swept
Her pride away and filled her with a song.

Quiescence

The night is panting across the hill,
The moon is tangerine,
The brassy earth is melting through
A drabby cloth of green.

And I am floating with a star
On a mauve and violet trail
Constructing a song. The cinnabar
Shoots up — O God, I must not fail.

Mystic of Grand Canyon

An infinite abyss of opal hills
    And fiery gods inverted a rainbow
On my sudden vision. The petty ills
    Of life dissolved, amazed as Queen Juno
I was transferred into a gypsy maze
    Of color. Drifting caverns wielded spears
Of silver mist that smote my wanton gaze
    And left a wanderlust for fleeting years.

The years have left a sweeter mystery
    Of love and tender hours, of laughter fused
With tawny shores and gilded ships at sea
    And moons of want-wit sadness. Still I mused
On drifting purples with a scarlet shade
    That taunted the lust of a gypsy maid.

Song of a Dying Hopi

You quenched the sacred birth fires
And spilled the yucca water
That purified the peaceful ones
In Walpi long ago.
Hopitu Shinumu O,
I am stricken, stricken low.

The ruins of gray pueblos
Are ashes on high mesas;
The tenderfoot is crushing the brave
Of Hopitu Shinumu.
God of my fathers save
Your son from a white-man-grave.

Paint my limbs in white of clay
And crimson of the sunset;
The sun will rise no more
For Hopitu Shinumu,
I see it sinking lower . . . lower . . .
Eagle Feather is no more.

A Sandstorm

A dreamy siren changed the budding land
    Into an Eden; through the languor a whine
Ascended with prophetic grains of sand
    As vivid rose revealed a head in line
With western sky and earth. A writhing flame
    Of dust was blown with reptile snorts of wrath
    And coils of anger flayed the rolling path
Of victory as dust imps overcame.

Deprived of sun and sky, the tree of life
    Became a sickly hue and dusty lint
Obscured each flower and swaying tree. A knife
    Of dust pierced Heaven through and pity bent
So near to earth, the serpent like a thief
Recoiled in shame and hid behind a leaf.

Reply to William Shakespeare

(Sonnet XVIII)

Do not compare me to a summer day
For I am built of storms and fire. A zone
Of tempests rules my heart, a minute stone,
A minute tears and then alackaday
My spirits rise to starry heights then flay
The dust with broken wings. Do not compare
Nor try to analyze my moods for there
Are those who tried and grievous did they pay.

And yet Laodamia could not be
More loyal nor summer more yielding than I
Have been to love and her delicious ways.
Compare me to the rain that furiously
And tremulously falls from the same sky
And to old wine and golden-headed maize.

Gypsy Night

My gypsy heart was livid with pain
And famished for a breath
Of cool west wind;

No lover came that torrid day
To cool my heart or cross
My palm with gain
Of gold.

I queried piteously,
Am I old? Am I old?

Then a western found my bed of moss
And amorous night descended;
They both entwined
Their arms about me
And kissed my world away.

Mortality

The thing
He made of dust
Presumes to doubt the sign
Of God in rose and morning star
And man.

Geraniums

The woman frail and princesslike was gray
Before her time, and pitiful to me
In faded garments as rapturously
She went about her tasks from day to day.

It mystified me for ashen her way
Appeared amid the drab obscurity
Of isolated monotony
Until I heard her pray:

Dear God, my thanks for life and gracious plans
And . . . rose geraniums in shining cans.

To a City

Audaciously you stand
With feet outspread,
A mighty beast
With pounding pulse.
You sniff and blow
And ebb and flow
Till dizzy is your head.
The world detests? No,
Hearts are quivering
While you are bled.

Beauty in Grief

My heart had reached the mountaintop before
I knew that grief unflinchingly as wind
Can sweep away capricious dreams. I bore
My youth at first with haughty pinions, blind
To sorrow but my heart dissolved its chains
And fled. I could not follow, brokenly
I lived but rugged stone nor slanting rains
Nor April buds meant anything to me.

I hated life, I hated love, forlorn
I walked alone, my heart had ceased to care
When grief impeccable as honeyed morn
Revealed itself to me and unaware
I was lifted to where my heart had trod,
And looked and found a beauty loving God.

Early Bug

Vinegar-ro-on
Diabolical despair
Of early settlers
Who lived in dugouts with you
But remained a mystery.

A Nightitude

The rain is falling drearily with gusts
Of autumn leaves. My children are away
For evening frolics and bitter thrusts
Of wind annoy the windows. Gone is day
And night intrudes with all her ragged train.
My only companion, my baby boy,
Is dreaming at my side. I must refrain
From reveries that will resurrect the joy
Of motherhood when baby laughter rang
Through every room. A lonely cock crows
And then — not another — left alone — BANG!
My baby jumps in his sleep. A mouse throws
A trap, my darling, be still and sleep away,
Dear lamb! Inaudible are the black hills;
The lights in the village below turn gray
And wink fantastically. Ghostly thrills
Of silver dreams propel the leaves apart
And rattle them as phantoms through my heart.
Another one here . . . a wasp on a beam . . .
My lids are heavy . . . I am forced to dream.

Autumn Speaks

At dawn the earth coquettishly
Spread her fan between the sky and me,
She blushed until a riot ran
Of blazing red behind her fan.
She called an artisan to her,
(I never saw such a conjurer)
"Regal Autumn is here," she said,
"Go bring my purples and my red."
Then with dexterous facility
She dyed the walnut and maple tree
In honey-combed-canary-gold.
Then reaching for her magic mold
She mixed a strange metallic blue
With madder rose, then deftly threw
The whole upon a mountainside
Which left the woods at eventide
An apricot and carmine glow
Reflecting ruby light below
On valleys locked in fond embrace.
I looked into her lovely face,
(My heart was pounding furiously)
I hugged my gypsy earth to me.

Tarantula

Tawny black invader of night
Your home is a spiral coil
Unillumined by the majestic light
Of Heaven. Your velveted toil
Is preceded by darkness; you know
Not the carmine and saffron and madder blue
Of a silver sky but stealthily go
Unheralded to the pit in lieu
With Shaitan: mundane shah
Of human fears — TARANTULA!

Penitence

He made a world and stars for me,
A flower, a song, and a willow tree,
And placed me here a little lower
Than angels; unbarred the door
Of Heaven and invited me there
To live in glory and to share
With Him a city of gold.
Today I saw a lily unfold
And a gorgeous sky of silver banks,
And forgot to give my Maker thanks.

Silver Wedding Anniversary

Today my dreams are fragrant with perfume
    Of valley lilies floating down an aisle
    Arm in arm with enchanted love and while
A heavenly Beethoven filled the room
Divine chanters whispered Amo Teum.
    Beneath a shining bell a voice echoed,
"To love, to honor and cherish for life";
    The magic words ran on and overflowed
With sweetness, "I pronounce you man and wife."

Amid the strains of Beethoven our hearts
    United to wage our battles with song
        And golden laughter. Then the awesome years
Submerged us in living and grievous arts
    That bruised our wings but made us ardent, strong,
        So now we reminisce through silver tears.

Friend

When others turned aside to jeer
With lifted brows and "Ohs!"
She walked a mile to meet me
And handed me a rose.

(In honor of Lucile Lacy)

Gins

The droning wheels are turning
Long before the disc is burning
Lakes of silver mauve to ruby fire
In the east. And higher still and higher
Lifts the smoke its ashen wings
Like promises of early springs
And violet mist and silver dawn.
Day in day out the wheels turn on.

The air is filled with choking lint
That gives the world a cotton tint.
A woman sees the smoke upcoil
And thinks of dreams and drouth and toil,
Of pallid hopes and aching backs,
Of children dragging heavy sacks,
Recalls the pearly clouds at dawn.
Day in day out the wheels turn on.

Across the field a farmer crawls
On burning knees and plucks the balls
Of snowy lint. He sees the smoke
And hears a mockingbird in an oak
And thinks with mingled hopes and fears
Of dreams he dreamed through empty years
And silver banks at early dawn.
Day in day out the wheels turn on.

Paulina

An amber string
Of Spanish beads
Their glory fling
Where hunger feeds.

Paulina knows
The punishment
But not the woes
Of penitent.

Sparkling and bright
They cling to her
As she sets right
The girl's dresser.

"Paulina, did
You see my string
Of beads amid
My gems nesting?"

Paulina shook
Her cunning head
And with a look,
"No sabe," said.

Earth Fools

He gave us portent acts to play on earth,
To you the man to me the role of love
And fragile womanhood; yours was of mirth
With granite touch, and mine the scorching worth
Of whitened faith. The unquenchable shove
Of primal urging kept you high above
The lacerated lowliness of birth
And I was humbled like the meekest dove.

At first we played our parts with skyward wings
As light as windflowers new blossomings,
But when the shades of death were subtly drawn
Upon the aftermath of shattered trust
And undisguised we truly looked upon
The roles we played as fools, we turned to dust.

My Emergency Kit

I went in search of beauty
And found that she had fled.
I ran a mile to catch her
And fell like one that's dead.

An angel took a shining key
And opened wide my heart,
Then wrapped it in a rainbow
That tied with magic art.

She placed it in a golden chest
And handed me the key;
I felt my pulses stir again
And rose up joyfully.

And now when beauty runs away,
I search not everywhere,
But open wide my treasure kit
And see a shining prayer.

Lupez

A crumbling adobe and a West Texas moon,
A thrumming guitar and an old Spanish tune,
Pedro is dreaming of a fair señorita,
Softly he is humming, "O más bonita!"
Lupez has a smile on her full young face
Tonight the old shack is a magical place.

On a dirty petate sits her beaming mama
And sprawled on the ground is her lazy papa
But a gay mantilla of fringes and lace
Matches the roses on Lupez' brown face.
Romping muchachos play over the yard
But Señor Don Pedro with a lover's regard
Sings on to Lupez of castles in Spain,
Of coquetting señoritas down Lover's Lane,
Of embroidered shawls his grandmother wore,
Of estancias he bought of a rich señor,
Of rambling haciendas with fuentes rare,
And Lupez was caught in the lover's old snare
In her crumbling adobe under a West Texas moon
With a thrumming guitar and an old Spanish tune.

An Easterner Describes a Ranch

I'll say, Mis' Jones, them renches
Out thar shore are fine,
I'll say they are.

People jes' ride erlong an' come
To them renches at eatin' time,
Yes, sir, Mis' Jones, I'll declar.
Jis' go in an' eat right thar,

Wunst when I wuz out to Menard
Well wunst when I wuz thar
With Elzy — he's my pard —
We rid right up at dinner time
No one to hum, we didn't keer a dime,
Elzy sez, "I'm hongry," and walked right in,
Whut did Elzy do? Jis' hepped hissef then
Opened some homebrew —
I declar hit's true.

Yes, sir, Mis' Jones, them renches is fine
When fo'ks is gone ter dinner time,
You kin walk in an' eat jis' the same,
No matter whut's your name.

Yes, sir, Mis' Jones, I'll sweer
I'd prove it by Elzy,
If he uz here.

Evanescence

At midnight I saw
Diagonal clouds submerge
The sky
And a golden splurge
Of a moon
Hanging by
A star,
And thought how soon
The glare of day
Would mar
This beauty
Then fade away.

Ingratitude

Upon the crooked elbow
Of a gnarled and ill-used tree
A cluster of mistletoe
Subsisted and a crow
Pecked tranquilly.

San Angelo

San Angelo, I lift the veil
Of time and see a silver trail
Of shining hoofs where buffalo
Once stalked to drink at new Concho
That sparkled then with strutting quail.

An Indian died without a wail,
A hut or two, a holy grail
Of life began to ebb and flow
San Angelo.

And like your west you could not fail
To hold your banner high. A tale
Of daring, golden faith and lo!
A jasper city that we know
As brotherly and time shall hail
San Angelo.

My Mustang

Little Mexican pony, when you were brought
To Texas by horse rustlers I wept
To see your star-winged pride.
Fires of untameable centuries swept
Their tempests through your span,
You knew nought
But to glide
In languid freedom.

You reared and plunged
When ruthless hands leashed you
As you lunged
Your heart against the grinding yoke of man.

I cringed at your proud nostrils' bloody foam
And quivering flesh slit open by leather thongs.
Your passionate spirit used to roam
Was slow to break as throngs
Of curses from your captors,
Seven,
Shouted, "Dam you shall be broke,
If not by us by Boger Red."

You felt the yoke
And plunged toward Heaven,
O my mustang; You . . . fell back . . . DEAD!

Spring Out West

I have a strange and restless longing
And desires that keep a-thronging
From the start.

For wild prairie winds are blowing
And the Concho is rippling, flowing
Miles apart.

For the song of windmills whirring
And the crux of blue quail stirring
Through my heart.

Old Bill

Old Bill was wont to reminisce on days
When he had felt the sting of arrows tipped
With steel or slept on the prairies always
Alert to danger and prowlers bloody lipped.

"I shall never forget that gruesome night,"
He said, "when Tejas ripped our Negro slave
Or Tonkawas in their pellmell flight . . .
Or when a cowboy went singing to his grave."

In time the folks grew tired of hours of this
And Bill was left alone to think and die.
But where Bill is I know that he will reminisce
For PIONEERS have golden harps in the sky.

Monarch of the Plains

In hair leggings, boots and spurs he rides
Into the rhythmic dawn of bournless day,
At his approach a prairie canine hides
Behind russet pyramids of clay.

He rides among his white-faced Hereford cows,
Their satin haunches dappled by the glow
Of an autumn sun. A lordly bull plows
The dust with silver hoofs and fierce bellow.

The rider glances at the Hereford bull
And notes with pride the muscled limbs
And sentient fire that make him terrible
To fence from scarlet lowings that stir his whims.

He misses a dogie calf from the herd
And rides until the dusky wings of night
Are flapping ghoulish shadows where stirred
Bloody prowlers now barking at his right.

He spurs his horse among the hungry pack
And lifts the calf in mercy to his breast,
Then furiously flees from the attack
Of baffled suckers and lure of the West.

Cowboy Song

I sing a song of bounding plains,
Siestas, spurs and bridle reins,
Hi yip hi yaddy hi ya hi ya
Hi yip hi yaddy hi ya.

I love the lure of cattle trails
Where daring courage never fails,
Hi yip hi yaddy hi ya hi ya
Hi yip hi yaddy hi ya.

A land of horns and shaggy hides
Where golden knighthood grandly rides,
Hi yip hi yaddy hi ya hi ya
Hi yip hi yaddy hi ya.

My lover wears a carmine rose
And tips the stars with his lassoes,
Hi yip hi yaddy hi ya hi ya
Hi yip hi yaddy hi ya.

Isidro the Shepherd

At dawn the tinkle tinkle of amber bells
Awakens the hombre Isidro;
He opens his eyes and counts the caravels
Of skurtling clouds: uno, dos, tres, cuatro —

His drowsy dog unslits an eye
Sabe mañana, Perro?
A gurgling flask is turned up high
An Indian fire begins to glow,
Sabe Borrachito?

He herds the nibbling sheep promiscuously
Intent on chasing a rainbow
Until in weary groups each finds a tree,
Isidro counts: uno, dos, tres, cuatro —

His lanky shepherd lolls nearby,
Sabe comida, Perro?
He dips tortillas in frijoles fry
And tilts his gay-banded sombrero,
Muy caliente! (Río?)

At night he sprawls beneath a yucca tree
And dreams he is a caballero
Alluring lovely señoritas: gallantly
He counts the stars: uno, dos, tres, cuatro —

His dog is fondling a butterfly,
Sabe amoroso, Perro?
Amber bells are tinkling a melody
Of love and stolen kisses . . . a banjo
Tenderly pleads: uno, dos, tres, cuatro —

Da Americano

(As Viewed by Pedro)

Da Mexicano he leeva in da lettla house;
When da weenda blow eet rocka dees way and dat.
Da Americano leeva in greata beega house
Weeth piano mas bonito, wan soft mat.

Mexicano no keepa da moneys wan day,
Da Americano he keepa hees alla time.
When Mexicano go to town he say
To muchachos, "Wanta da candee? Taka da dime."

Americano muchachos beg, "Papa, I wanta neekel
please."
Da papa he shaka da head, "No, no,
We must sava da moneys or we freeze.
Come on, we musta take da flours an' go."

Da Americano he steengy, he for hella go
When he coma for to die;
But da Mexicano he leeva in beega house
Away up inna da sky.

To a Writer Friend

O friend of my heart,
O friend of my soul,
O friend so far away,
I know you love
The things I love
For I read your book today.